5/00

W9-CYW-937

Wildlife Watching

Bat Watching

by Diane Bair and Pamela Wright

Consultant:
Denise R. Tomlinson
Director of Operations
Organization for Bat Conservation

CAPSTONE BOOKS
an imprint of Capstone Press
Mankato, Minnesota

Capstone Books are published by Capstone Press
P.O. Box 669, 151 Good Counsel Drive, Mankato, Minnesota 56002
http://www.capstone-press.com

Library of Congress Cataloging-in-Publication Data
Bair, Diane.
    Bat watching/by Diane Bair and Pamela Wright.
    p. cm.—(Wildlife watching)
    Includes bibliographical references (p. 44) and index.
    Summary: Describes the physical characteristics and behavior of bats, different
species, and how to safely observe them.
    ISBN 0-7368-0318-1
    1. Bat watching—Juvenile literature. [1. Bat watching. 2. Bats.] I. Wright, Pamela,
1953– . II. Title. III. Series.
QL737.C5B25   2000
599.4—dc21
                                                                    99–19606
                                                                    CIP

Editorial Credits
Carrie A. Braulick, editor; Steve Christensen, cover designer and illustrator;
    Heidi Schoof, photo researcher

Photo Credits
David F. Clobes, cover inset, 18, 21, 39
Gary Milburn/TOM STACK & ASSOCIATES, 11
International Stock/Ronn Maratea, 40 (bottom)
Jeff Foott/TOM STACK & ASSOCIATES, 26
Joe McDonald, cover
Joe McDonald/TOM STACK & ASSOCIATES, 12, 40 (top)
Merlin D. Tuttle, 17, 41 (top), 42 (top), 42 (bottom)
Michael P. Turco, 47
Rob and Ann Simpson, 4, 36, 41 (bottom)
Robert and Linda Mitchell, 6, 32
Thomas Kitchin/TOM STACK & ASSOCIATES, 9
Unicorn Stock Photos/Marshall Prescott, 22
Visuals Unlimited/Rob Simpson, 24; Richard C. Johnson, 29; Bill Beatty, 35

**Thank you to Bob Benson, Bat Conservation International, for his assistance in
preparing this book.**

Table of Contents

Chapter 1

Getting to Know Bats

Some people are afraid of bats. But these people probably do not understand bats. Bats are not dangerous creatures. You can go bat watching to learn more about bats. Bats can be fascinating to observe in the wild.

The Truth about Bats

Many people have false ideas about bats. For example, some people believe bats drink blood. But this is only true of vampire bats. These bats live in Central and South America. Vampire bats feed on the blood of animals

Many people do not understand bats.

Vampire bats live in Central and South America.

such as cattle, horses, and birds. They rarely
feed on the blood of people.

Other people believe bats will fly into
their hair. But most bats try to avoid people.
One scientist tested whether bats will stay in
hair. He tried to make a bat stay on a person's
head. He even wrapped hair around the bat.
But the bat did not stay on the person's head.

Some people think all bats spread rabies. This serious disease can affect the brains and spinal cords of animals and people. It may cause death. Animals that have rabies spread the disease through their bites. Bats can spread rabies. But bats usually do not bite unless they are touched. Scientists have found that less than .5 percent of all bats have rabies.

About Bats

Bats are mammals. Mammals are warm-blooded animals. Their body temperature remains about the same in all surroundings. Young mammals drink milk produced by their mothers. Bats are the only mammals that fly.

Nearly 1,000 different types of bats live in the world. Each type of bat is called a species. Bats have more species than almost any other mammal. Only rodents have more species than bats. The rodent group includes rats and gophers. Forty-five bat species live in the United States and Canada.

Bats have different living habits from many other animals. They are nocturnal. This means they are more active at night. You may see bats hunt for food at night. Bats live in roosts during the day. Bats rest and sleep in these places. Some bats have roosts on cave ceilings or tree branches. Others live in attics or old mines. Bats hang upside down when they rest and sleep in their roosts.

Microbats and Megabats

People divide bats into two groups. These groups are microbats and megabats.

Most bats are microbats. Microbats are small. They have small eyes and large ears. Almost all microbats eat insects. But some microbats eat other food such as nectar. Flowering plants produce this sweet liquid. Microbats also may eat fruit or small animals such as lizards or birds. Vampire bats belong to the microbat group. Microbats live in many places around the world. But they do not live in areas that have very hot or cold climates.

Megabats are larger than microbats. They have large eyes and small ears. These bats can see better than microbats. Megabats eat plant

Bats hang upside down in their roosts.

8

parts. Most megabats eat fruit or nectar. Megabats only live in tropical regions of the world. Australia and southeast Asia have large populations of megabats. Many megabats also live in tropical areas of Africa and India.

Helpful Bats

False beliefs have made bats unpopular with many people. But bats are helpful creatures. Some bats spread pollen. These tiny yellow grains stick to bats' fur when bats eat nectar from plants. Bats then bring the pollen to other plants. Many of these plants need pollen so they can reproduce.

Some bats eat fruit. Many of these fruits have seeds. Bats often swallow the seeds. But bats cannot digest seeds. They get rid of the seeds in their droppings when they fly from plant to plant. Bats also may spit the seeds out when they eat fruit. These seeds grow into new plants. Bats spread about 95 percent of the seeds in the world's rainforests.

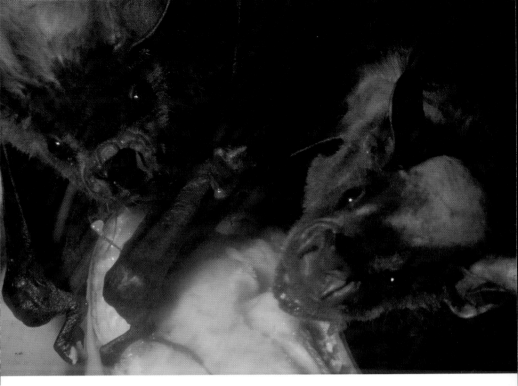

Some bats eat fruit.

Many bats eat insects. Some insects are harmful to crops and bothersome to people. Bats that eat these insects help make people more comfortable and keep crops healthy.

Some people use bat droppings for fertilizer. These droppings are called guano. People gather guano from bat roosts or purchase it. They then put the guano on soil to help their plants and crops grow.

Amazing Bat Abilities

Microbats have some special abilities. These bats use echolocation to find food and avoid objects in the dark.

Microbats echolocate by making sounds through their noses or mouths. Most of these sounds are above people's range of hearing. When the sounds hit an object, the echoes bounce back to the bats. The echoes tell bats that an object is near.

Microbats can recognize the sizes and shapes of objects through echolocation. They can even recognize insect types. For example, they sense if an insect is a mosquito or a moth.

Megabats do not use echolocation. These bats mainly rely on their excellent eyesight and sense of smell to find food.

Bats have other unusual abilities. They can eat large amounts of food for their size. Bats may eat as much as their body weight in food in one day. Some microbats eat as many as 3,000 insects in a night. A bat species called the little brown bat can eat about 1,200 insects in one hour.

Microbats make sounds through their noses or mouths when they echolocate.

Endangered Bats

Bats are disappearing around the world. More than half of the bats in the United States are in decline or endangered. Species that have decreasing populations are in decline. Endangered animal species may soon die out.

Bats are in trouble for many reasons. Some bats are trapped and die when people close caves or old mines. Some bats lose their roosts when people cut down trees. Some people kill bats that have roosts in their houses or buildings.

Some bats are poisoned by chemicals people use to protect wood on buildings. Bats that live in these buildings sometimes absorb the chemicals through their skin. They then may become sick and die.

Pesticides also harm bat populations. Pesticides are chemicals that people spray on plants and crops to kill insects. Some bats eat insects that have pesticides in them. These bats can die from pesticide poisoning. Pesticides also make it harder for bats to find insects to eat.

Removing Bats from Buildings

Bats sometimes have roosts in buildings. People sometimes kill these bats. But people can remove bats from buildings without harming them. They can follow these steps to safely remove the bats.

1. Identify where bats enter and leave buildings. Watch the bats leave the buildings in early evening.

2. Place a piece of bird netting or window screen over any openings bats use. Cover the openings entirely.

3. Tape the netting or screen with duct tape on all sides of openings except the bottom. This creates a one-way exit.

4. Leave the netting or screen up for at least a week. This helps make sure that bats are not trapped inside.

5. Close up the openings so bats cannot enter again.

People should remove bats in early spring or late summer. Young bats that cannot fly may be trapped in roosts if bats are removed during other times. Some people put bat houses up near their homes before they remove bats. Bats may then use the houses for new roosts.

Many people try to protect bats. Some people put special gates on caves and old mines. The gates keep people out and allow bats to enter. Some people teach others how to remove bats from buildings. Other people build bat houses. These houses provide bats with roosts. You can learn how to build a bat house.

Build a Bat House

You can build a bat house to provide a roost for bats. This may allow you to observe bats near your home. It also can help protect bat populations.

1. Try to locate your bat house near a water source such as a stream, river, or lake. Bats eat many insects that live in these areas.

2. Place your bat house in a sunny spot. Bats prefer warm roosts.

3. Use rough or grooved wood in the inside of your bat house. This allows bats to grip the wood.

4. Place your bat house as high as possible. It should be placed at least 15 to 20 feet (4.6 to 6 meters) high. This protects bats from predators such as cats, weasels, and snakes.

5. Mount your bat house on the sides of buildings or poles. Bat houses on trees may receive too much shade. These houses may become too cool for bats.

6. Do not use chemicals to treat wood on your bat house. Bats may absorb these chemicals through their skin and become sick.

7. Paint your bat house dark brown or black if you live in an area with a cool or moderate climate. Paint your bat house medium-brown to white if you live in a hot climate. This helps provide bats with proper roost temperatures.

8. Line your bat house with fiberglass or plastic window screening. This helps young bats grip the tops of your bat house. Do not use metal screening. This screening becomes too hot. It may burn bats' feet.

9. Make sure the wood on your bat house fits together tightly. Gaps in the wood may let in drafts. Bats may become too cold in these drafty bat houses.

Locate the following resources for more information about how to build a bat house:

Bat Conservation Society of Oklahoma
http://www.batcon.org/bhra/bhratop.html

North American Bat House Research Project
http://members.aol.com/bcsok/housplan.jpg

Gelfand, Dale E. *Building Bat Houses.* A Storey Country Wisdom Bulletin. Pownal, Vt.: Storey Pub., 1997.

Mullins, Will. *A Bat House in Every Yard: How to Control Mosquitoes and Other Pests around Your Home or Farm with Nature's Pest Patrol.* St. Peters, Mo.: Wilco Pub., 1997.

Tuttle, Merlin D. and Donna L. Hensley. *The Bat House Builder's Handbook.* Austin, Texas: Bat Conservation International, 1993.

Chapter 2

Preparing for Your Adventure

Learn more about bats before you go bat watching. Check out books about bats from your school or local library. You may want to check out bat field guides. These books show what bats look like and tell where they live. This book has a short field guide on pages 40 to 42.

When to Go Bat Watching

Summer is the best time to see bats. Many bats have difficulty finding food during winter. These bats often hibernate or migrate. Bats that hibernate find hidden roosts and go into a

You may want to check out books to learn more about bats.

deep sleep. They wake and become active again in spring. Bats that migrate fly to warm places to live during winter.

Bat watching is an evening activity. Bats usually come out to eat at sundown.

What to Bring

You should bring a flashlight and extra batteries when you go bat watching. The flashlight will help you see bats in the dark. Point the flashlight toward the sky and move it around to look for bats.

A bat detector also is useful for bat watching. This small electronic device allows you to easily hear bats' echolocation calls. The detector will help you discover whether there are bats in your area. You may be able to purchase a bat detector from bat conservation organizations. These groups work to protect bats.

Other items also can be helpful for bat watching. Bring an extra jacket and insect repellent. You may be outside for a long period of time. You could become hungry or thirsty. You may want to bring a snack and water. Be sure to

A flashlight can help you see bats in the dark.

take home any containers, wrappers, and other items that you bring with you. This helps protect the land and water against pollution.

You may want to bring supplies to record bat information. Bring a notebook and a pen. You may want to bring a bat field guide. A sketch pad may be helpful to draw bats. You may want a tape recorder to record bat calls.

Safety

Bat watchers need to follow some important safety rules. Children should go bat watching with an adult. Adults can help guide children so that they do not become lost at night.

You should never touch bats. Bats may bite if they are handled. Always stay away from bats on the ground. These bats may be sick.

Pay attention to your surroundings. There may be other animals in your area. Try not to disturb these animals. Look for landmarks as you walk. You may see logs or trail signs. You can use these landmarks to find your way home.

Some safety rules help protect bats. Never bother sleeping or hibernating bats in their roosts. Sleeping bats need to save their energy to find food at night. Hibernating bats need to conserve their energy to survive until spring. A hibernating bat that is awakened may lose 10 to 30 days of energy.

Hibernating bats must rest to conserve their energy.

Chapter 3

Where to Look

Look for bats in their habitats. These are the places and natural conditions in which bats live. Bats have food and roosts in their habitats.

Different bat species have different habitats. Some bats live in forests or near streams or lakes. Bats usually are not found on prairies. These flat, grassy areas have few trees. Prairies do not provide bats with enough protection from predators. Predators hunt other animals for food. Some bat predators include owls, raccoons, and snakes.

Look for different bat species in their ranges. These are the geographic regions where a plant or animal species naturally lives. For example,

Some bats live in forests.

Most North American bats eat insects.

the range of the Mexican free-tailed bat
includes the southern parts of North America.

Feeding Areas
Look for bats as they hunt for food. Bats feed
at sundown during clear and warm weather.
They usually stay in their roosts on cold or
rainy nights. Look for bats feeding in open

areas. Parks with wide, open spaces are good places to look for bats.

Other areas also attract hunting bats. Bats often appear near streetlights in cities. Light attracts insects that bats eat. Look for bats near forest edges. Bats often feed on the plentiful supply of insects in forests. You may find bats near ponds, rivers, or lakes. You may see these bats dive down to drink water.

Scan the sky with your flashlight when you look for bats. Some bats fly low to eat. They may land to pick up beetles or other insects. Other bats fly high and straight. These bats feed on flying mosquitoes and moths.

You may see nectar-eating bats if you live in the southwestern United States. Look for these bats near flower gardens at night. You also may find nectar-eating bats near hummingbird feeders. These bats are attracted to the sweet, nectar-like liquid that people place in the feeders.

Roosts

You also can look for bats near their roosts. Bats live in roosts by themselves or in groups. Bats that live by themselves are called solitary bats. Solitary bats have roosts in hidden places. They may hang in the leaves of trees or crawl behind tree bark. Some of these bats live under loose shingles in buildings or in hollow trees.

A group of bats living together is called a colony. Some bat colonies include nearly 1 million bats. Bat colonies may live in caves, attics, or barns. Some colonies also live in abandoned mines.

Bats leave their roosts during the evening to hunt for food. This is called a bat emergence. Bat emergences are good opportunities to see many bats. But bats may stay inside their roosts during unfavorable weather.

Never disturb bat roosts. You should be as quiet as possible near roosts. Do not shine a flashlight at roosts. Never enter bat roosts.

You may see many bats during a bat emergence.

Places to See Bats

1 **Carlsbad Caverns National Park, Carlsbad, New Mexico:**
This park has emergences of about 300,000 Mexican free-tailed bats from the end of May to the end of October. Visitors view bats from an amphitheater. Visitors also may attend a park ranger's talk about bats.

2 **Blowing Wind Cave National Wildlife Refuge, Decatur, Alabama:**
This refuge has emergences of Indiana and gray bats during summer.

3 **Selman Bat Cave, Wildlife Management Viewing Area, near Woodward, Oklahoma:**
This area has emergences of 500,000 to 1 million Mexican free-tailed bats during late summer. Visitors may view bats with a guide.

4 **Congress Avenue Bridge, Austin, Texas:**
Visitors can see emergences of about 1 million Mexican free-tailed bats at this bridge during summer.

5 **Canoe Creek State Park, Hollidaysburg, Pennsylvania:**
Emergences of little brown bats take place here from May through October. Bat programs are available.

6 **Rushing River Provincial Park, Kenora, Ontario, Canada:**
This park has emergences of little brown bats during summer. Bat programs are available.

7 **Nickajack Cave Wildlife Refuge, Marion County, Tennessee:**
Emergences of about 50,000 endangered gray bats occur here from late April through early October. Visitors can view the bats from a viewing platform.

8 **Grand Canyon National Park, Grand Canyon, Arizona:**
Visitors can see a variety of bat species throughout this park during evenings. Many western pipistrelle bats live in the park.

Public Viewing Areas

You may want to visit places that are well-known for their bat populations. Many wildlife refuges and state and national parks in the United States and Canada have large bat colonies.

Some of these bat viewing places offer tours. Guides can show you the best viewing areas on tours. They may teach you about the bats in the area. Some places have bat programs. You may see films or listen to speeches about bats during these programs.

Chapter 4

Making Observations

Be patient while you look for bats. You may have to go out several nights in order to see bats. Bats stay in their roosts on some nights. Learn what to look for when you go bat watching. This will help you recognize bats and their signs.

Bat Wings

All bats have features you can note when you go bat watching. Look at bats' wings. Their wings are very large compared to their bodies. Bats' wings can be four times the size of their bodies. Some large bats have a wingspan of

Some bats have very large wingspans.

6 feet (1.8 meters). The largest wingspan of North American bats is about 2 feet (.6 meter).

The scientific name for bats is Chiroptera (kye-ROP-tar-uh). This Greek word means hand-wing. Bats' wings are similar to people's hands. Each wing has four long fingers and one short thumb. Bats have strong skin that stretches across these fingers. They do not have feathers on their wings like birds.

Bats' thumbs look like claws. One thumb sticks out from each wing. Bats use their sharp thumbs to grip smooth surfaces.

Bat Guano

Look for guano to find out if bats are in your area. Look for small, round pellets. Bat guano is about the size of a grain of rice. You may see large piles of bat guano on the ground or floor beneath bat roosts. Look for bat guano near bat houses.

Do not touch guano with your hands. This can spread disease.

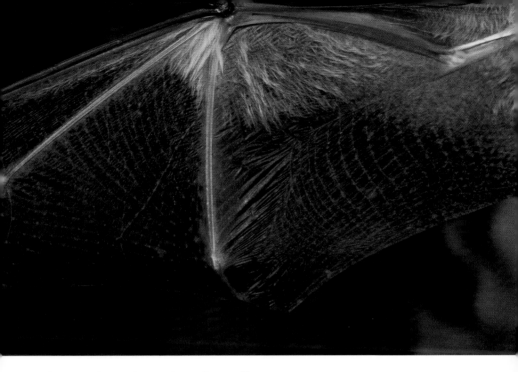

Bats' wings have four long fingers.

Listening for Bat Calls
Listen for bat calls when you go bat watching. It is easiest to hear bat calls with a bat detector. A bat detector may even allow you to identify different bat species. For example, red bats make chirping sounds. Big brown bats make buzzing sounds. Little brown bats make ticking sounds. All of these bats live in North America.

It may be difficult to identify different bat species from their sounds at first. But you may learn these sounds as you gain bat watching experience.

You may hear bat calls without a bat detector. Bats often call out to each other in their roosts. These calls are not the same as echolocation calls. Remember not to disturb bats if you hear them in their roosts.

You may hear the echolocation calls of some large bat species without a bat detector. For example, hoary bats and mastiff bats make loud clicking sounds. Hoary bats live throughout southern Canada and most of the United States. Mastiff bats live in the southwestern United States.

Bat and Bird Differences

People sometimes mistake bats for birds. There are a few ways to tell them apart. Birds usually place their wings close to their bodies while they fly. Bats keep their wings pointed outward during flight. Birds fly smoothly. Bats have

You may hear bats call out in their roosts.

37

jerky flight patterns. Birds rarely fly after sundown. But bats head out to eat at that time.

You may see nighthawks after dark. These birds catch insects at night like bats do. They usually fly near well-lit areas. But nighthawks are much larger than most North American bats. They also have stripes on their wings. Bats do not have stripes on their wings.

Recording Your Observations

Record important information about the bats you observe. You can use this information as you continue to watch bats. You may write this information in a notebook. For example, you can note bats' colors and wingspans. You may note whether they are living in colonies or alone. You can write down the days and times of bat emergences.

You may be able to make sketches of bats if there is enough light. Try to draw all parts of the bats.

Take notes about bats each time you go bat watching. This will help you learn even more about bats.

You may want to record your bat observations.

North American Field Guide

Little Brown Bat

Description: Little brown bats are one of the most common bats in North America. These bats have brown, glossy fur and long, narrow ears. Little brown bats are about 3 inches (7.6 centimeters) long. These bats have roosts in caves, mines, buildings, or hollow trees. Little brown bats hibernate during the winter.

Habitat: Near streams, rivers, or lakes

Food: Insects, often mosquitoes

■ = Range

Big Brown Bat

Description: Big brown bats have a wide North American range. These bats have features similar to little brown bats. But big brown bats are larger. They are about 4 inches (10 centimeters) long. Big brown bats often have roosts in buildings. Most big brown bats live in small colonies. These bats often hibernate in caves, mines, attics, and buildings.

Habitat: Meadows; near fields, pastures, lakes, or rivers

Food: Insects, often beetles

■ = Range

Red Bat

Description: Red bats have long, orange-red fur with white spots on their wrists and shoulders. Females are a paler color than males. Red bats have short, rounded ears. These bats are about 4 inches (10 centimeters) long. Most red bats migrate to the southern United States and Mexico in the fall. Red bats are solitary bats. They have roosts in trees. Red bats are fast fliers compared to most other bat species.

Habitat: Forests

Food: Insects, often moths

 = Range

Hoary Bat

Description: Hoary bats are yellow-brown with white-tipped fur. Their tail membranes are entirely furred. Their ears are edged in black. Hoary bats have yellow-orange throat collars. They may look silver in flight. These bats are about 5 inches (13 centimeters) long. Hoary bats are solitary. They often have roosts in evergreen trees. Most hoary bats migrate south in fall.

Habitat: Forests, near forest edges

Food: Insects, often moths

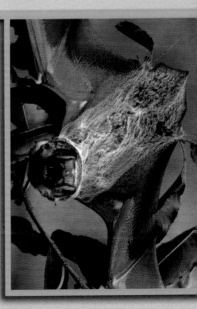

= Range

Mexican Free-Tailed Bat

Description: Mexican free-tailed bats have dark brown or gray velvety fur. They have long tails that extend beyond the skin that connects their legs and tails. Their large, rounded ears almost join at the middle of their foreheads. Mexican free-tailed bats are about 3 inches (7.6 centimeters) long. These bats migrate south to Mexico and Central America for winter. They form very large colonies. Mexican free-tailed bats often have roosts in caves. But they also can be found in buildings or under bridges.

Habitat: Meadows, fields, near rivers and lakes

Food: Insects, often moths

■ = Range

Silver-Haired Bat

Description: Silver-haired bats are black or dark brown with silver-tipped fur. They usually are about 3 inches (7.6 centimeters) long. These bats are solitary. But female silver-haired bats may raise their young with other female bats in small colonies. Silver-haired bats have roosts on tree branches in forests or under loose tree bark. Many silver-haired bats migrate south for the winter. Silver-haired bats are sometimes mistaken for hoary bats. But hoary bats usually are larger than these bats.

Habitat: Forests; along ponds, streams, and lakes

Food: Variety of small insects

■ = Range

Words to Know

echolocation (ek-oh-loh-KAY-shuhn)—the process of using sound and echoes to locate objects and food; microbats use echolocation to hunt for insects.

guano (GWAH-no)—bat droppings or waste

habitat (HAB-uh-tat)—the natural places and conditions in which an animal lives

hibernate (HYE-bur-nate)—to go into a deep sleep during winter

migrate (MYE-grate)—to move from one area to another as the seasons change

nocturnal (nok-TUR-nuhl)—to be active at night

predator (PRED-uh-tur)—an animal that hunts other animals for food

range (RAYNJ)—geographic region where a plant or animal species naturally lives

roost (ROOST)—a place where bats rest

To Learn More

Ackerman, Diane. *Bats: Shadows in the Night.* New York: Crown Publishers, 1997.

Arnold, Caroline. *Bat.* New York: Morrow Jr. Books, 1996.

Graham, Gary L. *Bats of the World.* Golden Guide. New York: Golden Books, 1994.

Lundberg, Kathryn T. *Bats for Kids.* Wildlife for Kids. Minocqua, Wis.: NorthWord Press, 1996.

Williams, Kim and Rob Mies. *Understanding Bats: Discovering the Secret Lives of These Gentle Mammals.* Marietta, Ohio: Bird Watcher's Digest Press, 1996.

Useful Addresses

Basically Bats
6146 Fieldcrest Drive
Morrow, GA 30260

Bat Conservation International
P.O. Box 162603
Austin, TX 78716

The Bat Conservation Society of Canada
P.O. Box 56042, Airways Postal Outlet
Calgary, AB T2E 8K5
Canada

Organization for Bat Conservation
1553 Haslett Road
Haslett, MI 48840

Internet Sites

Aerodynamics of Bats
http://muttley.ucdavis.edu/Book/Animals/
   intermediate/bats-01.html

Bat Conservation International
http://www.batcon.org

Bats4Kids
http://members.aol.com/bats4kids

Canadian Bat Resources
http://www.cancaver.ca/bats

Organization for Bat Conservation
http://www.batconservation.org

Index